D1612504

The Penalty Kick

Daniel Memmert & Benjamin Noël

THE PENALTY KICK

The Psychology of Success

MEYER & MEYER SPORT

British Library Cataloguing in Publication Data
A catalogue record for this book is available from the British Library

Original title: *Elfmeter: Die Psychologie des Strafstoßes*, © 2017 by Hogrefe Verlag GmbH & Co. KG

The Penalty Kick
Maidenhead: Meyer & Meyer Sport (UK) Ltd., 2020
ISBN: 978-1-78255-194-2

Aachen, Auckland, Beirut, Cairo, Cape Town, Dubai, Hägendorf, Hong Kong, Indianapolis, Manila, New Delhi, Singapore, Sydney, Tehran, Vienna

Member of the World Sports Publishers' Association (WSPA) www.w-s-p-a.org
Printed by Versa Press, East Peoria, IL, USA
ISBN: 978-1-78255-194-2
Email: info@m-m-sports.com
www.thesportspublisher.com

CONTENTS

FOREWORD

Penalties and penalty shootouts are very special situations: There is a lot of adrenaline, stress, rush, stage fright, thrill, tension—and fun.

In my role as a national goalkeeper coach, I am lucky enough to work with some of the greatest, world-class goalkeepers. My aspiration is to develop "my boys" through making use of imminent and innovative playing methods.

The FIFA World Cup 2006 in Germany demonstrated the importance of meticulous preparation and the right training for goalkeepers. This information on the now well-known note helped Jens Lehmann in the penalty shootout against Argentina, and was the sole reason for the match later being labeled as the "summer fairy tale." Back then, we still used tallies and just processed all of the information that was handed to us. However, today we use a database which presents all penalty takers alongside their preferred shot directions and shot strategies. This allows me to make quantitative and qualitative observations and then pass them on in a structured manner. Moreover, this enables my protégés to make up their own mind about their opponents and scorers.

There are many myths surrounding the penalty kick. In fact, I am often confronted with diverse theories, and continually asked about the way that the goalkeeper should behave. Should he draw the scorer's attention to him? Should he perform deceptive movements? Should he jump toward the left side if the scorer kicks the ball with his right foot? Should the goalkeeper try to appear "tall?" And if so, how? Should he remain standing for a long time? Should he offer one corner? After being bombarded with questions, I often wonder if anyone has the answers.

This is where this book can help. The authors were able to bring light into the darkness and present saved results on penalty shootouts. The sports science results on this research area are remarkable, making it apparent that it is not just soccer practice that stimulates soccer science, but rather that it works both ways. The next step would be to consolidate practice recommendations from these results in order to elaborate games and trainings and bring innovation to the training ground.

Dear soccer friends, I hope you enjoy reading this book, and I wish you good luck for the world's most wonderful side activity.

–Andreas Köpke

National goalkeeper coach of "Die Mannschaft"

INTRODUCTION

Penalty shootouts determine the outcome of games and are therefore both fascinating and meaningful in soccer, from grass roots up to the UEFA Champions League. This is the reason why penalty kicks interest a large amount of viewers, fans, media, athletes, and teams. It is highly probable that for upcoming events, we will experience individual penalty kicks in preliminary round matches, or penalty shootouts in knockout matches will decide whether a team drops out or advances to the next round. This will cause whole nations to either drown in grief or express their exuberant excitement in a parade, turning it into something that will go on to be remembered for a long time.

During the 2016 Rio Olympics men's final, a true penalty kick thriller occurred in the Maracanã stadium. The German soccer team lost against Brazil 5-6 in a penalty shootout. During regular play, Neymar gave his team the lead, but Max Meyer then went on to score in the second half. In the final penalty shootout, Nils Petersen was the only scorer who missed, allowing Neymar to solidify Brazil's victory. Since 1976, almost every fifth knockout match of the FIFA World Cup or the UEFA European Championship has been decided by a penalty shootout. There's a 60% chance that the future FIFA World or FIFA European leader will have to engage in a penalty shootout on its way to claim the title.

In the last 30 years, more than 120 scientific studies have tried to identify factors which influence the success of a penalty kick. In this popular science book, we present the knowledge of penalty shootouts which can easily be understood by players, trainers, and even the average soccer fan. We do not, however, neglect consolidated research results in sports psychology and the movement science. Sports scientific presentations, which are commonly not readily available to the public, are connected and processed "easily and loosely" with historical soccer dramas. It is more about common statements about the shot and point, than about outstanding scorers' or goalkeepers' performances. For example, we do not try to clarify why Jean-Marie Pfaff has the best rate in the German Bundesliga, with 66% of saved penalty shots (10 were saved out of 15 on the post apart from the goal). Likewise, we do not explain why Hans Joachim Abel has been able to convert all of his 16 penalty shots and, thereby become the best penalty taker in the history of the Bundesliga (besides Manfred Kaltz, who has the most converted penalty shootouts, however with "only" a rate of 88%). From the goalkeeper's viewpoint, we do not question why certain penalty shootout killers, like Robert Enke who saved 9 out of 18 penalty kicks, exist. The success probability is an unbelievable 50%, with only every fourth penalty kick being held. We also do not question why successful goalkeepers exist, goalkeepers like Hans Jörg Butt who not only saved 14, but also scored 26 (3 of them in the UEFA Champions-League).

In the penalty shootout, two people are always the focus: the kicker and the goalkeeper. We have therefore divided our chapters according to these two roles and have explored individual time phases before the kick for both of them. Furthermore, we have chosen current and historical stories which should clarify how sports science can possibly explain past dramatic shootouts.

However, when viewing the scientific data, it becomes increasingly apparent that many performance aspects of penalty shootouts are not sufficiently explored. This can be the reason for why few hedged findings have made their way onto the training ground, and hardly any systematic intervention measurements exist to improve the performance in penalty kicks. Therefore, we continue to hear the phrase "penalty shootouts cannot be trained!" One of the greatest German coaches, Jupp Heynckes (Champions League success with Real Madrid 1998 and FC Bayern München 2013) has even referred to penalty shootouts as "lottery games." The pressure of the game cannot be reconstructed, as with the physical and psychological exhaustion after 120 minutes. However, more than 120 sports science studies show that the probability of successfully scoring from the point can be optimized, and penalties, corner kicks, or free kicks can therefore be systematically trained.

The phenomenon of the penalty shootout is examined in this book from different and interesting approaches. Whether or not these findings can be implemented at the next FIFA World Cup is doubtful. In any case, we all hope that our national teams successfully take part in the FIFA World Cup, with or without penalty kicks.

REFERENCES

Dicks, M., Uehara, L., & Lima, C. (2011). Deception, individual differences and penalty kicks: Implications for goalkeeping in Association Football. International Journal of Sports Science & Coaching, 6, 515-521. DOI: 10.1260/1747-9541.6.4.515

Froese, G. (2012). Sportpsychologische Einflussfaktoren der Leistung von Elfmeterschützen. Hamburg: Verlag Dr. Kovač.

Lees, A., Asai, T., Andersen, T. B., Nunome, H., & Sterzing, T. (2010). The biomechanics of kicking in soccer: A review. Journal of Sports Sciences, 28, 805-817. DOI: 10.1080/02640414.2010.481305

Memmert, D., Hüttermann, S., Hagemann, N., Loffing, F., & Strauss, B. (2013). Dueling in the penalty box: Evidence-based recommendations on how penalty takers and goalkeepers can win penalty shootouts in soccer. International Review of Sport and Exercise Psychology, 6, 209-229.

Jordet, G., Hartman, E., Visscher, C., & Lemmink, K. (2007). Kicks from the penalty mark in soccer: The roles of stress, skill, and fatigue for kick outcomes. Journal of Sports Sciences, 25 (2), 121-129.

Starting Conditions Before the Penalty Shootout

Will the team with the first shot win the penalty shootout?

There is a well-known myth about penalty shootouts during knockout matches: The team taking the first penalty kick is assumed to have a better possibility of winning the competition. There are many examples from international tournaments, such as during the European Championship 2012 in Poland and Ukraine. England lost 2-4 against Italy in penalty kicks after Italy's Mario Balotelli took the first penalty. Another example is the semi-final between Portugal and Spain; Spain started and won 2-4.

The team taking the second shot often has to score to equalize, so there is always more pressure on their penalty kick. If they miss the second shot, they risk falling behind and losing the game.

From the DFB Cup in Germany in 1986 and 2006, 95 penalty shootouts were analyzed to test whether having the first shot during penalty shootouts was an advantage. This totaled to

1,009 penalty kicks. Apart from the overall outcome after a penalty shootout (victory vs. defeat), the team that went first was also noted (team: 1st shot, team: 2nd shot). However, it was discovered that this first team had no significant advantage over their opponents. After the penalty shootout, the team that started with the first penalty kick won the match in 48% of all penalty shootouts, but this does not statistically differ from 50%. Hence, having the first shot in a penalty shootout does not seem to provide a psychological advantage.

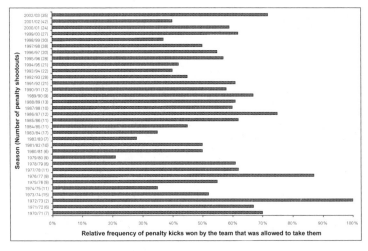

Figure 1. Shows how often the team with the first shot has won a penalty shootout for every season since 1970/71. The data set includes FIFA World Championships, Continental Championships, and the most significant European Club Cup Tournaments (national/international). Together, this was 709 penalty kick scenarios, with the number of penalties per season shown in brackets.

REFERENCES

Kocher M. G., Lenz M. V., & Sutter M. (2008). Performance under pressure — The case of penalty shootouts in football. In Andersson P., Ayton P. & Schmidt C. (eds.) *Myths and Facts About Football: The Economics and Psychology of the World's Greatest Sport* (S. 61-72). Newcastle: Cambridge Scholars Publishing.

Kocher M. G., Lenz M. V., & Sutter M. (2012). Psychological pressure in competitive environments: New evidence from randomized natural experiments. *Management Science, 58*, 1585-1591.

Is there a home field advantage in penalty shootouts?

Finals of the UEFA Champions League, World Cups, or European Championships are normally carried out on neutral ground. An exception to this was the nearly legendary UEFA Champions League final in 2012 during which FC Bayern Munich played against FC Chelsea at home in the Allianz Arena on May 19. This was referred to as "*Finale dahoam*" (Bavarian for "final at home") in the Bavarian capital. The score was 1-1 after 120 minutes, and FC Chelsea defeated Bayern Munich in penalty kicks, winning their first UEFA Champions League title. German national player, Bastian Schweinsteiger, was not able to convert the fifth shot, with his kick hitting the goal post. Due to the outcome of the penalty shootout and the missed opportunity of winning the Champions League at home, the event was eventually called "*Drama dahoam*" ("drama at home").

But did the home team lose the penalty shootout despite having the home field advantage? A well-known myth regarding penalty shootouts is that the home team has a greater chance of winning a penalty shootout. This is controversial but has been discussed in sport science publications over the past few years. From a sport psychological perspective, there are two questions that must be asked: Can the large number of supporters for the home team as well as the familiar environment be considered an advantage? Do higher expectations of the home team's fans lead to higher pressure on the home team?

The 95 penalty kicks were analyzed to answer whether a home field advantage during penalty shootouts exists. These all took place between 1986 and 2006 during the DFB Cup. Both the location (home game vs. away game) and the respective outcome of penalty shootouts (victory vs. defeat) were included. However, there was no significant home field advantage evident during penalty shootouts. A different analysis showed that the pressure that is placed on both teams to "sustain" is significant, and should therefore be taken into consideration when analyzing the home field advantage. During the first rounds of the DFB Cup, amateur teams always have the right to play at home. However, although the better teams are more often the away teams, the home teams are still likely to win. In later rounds, where the teams are equally as strong, the home teams are often more likely to lose.

An analysis of 365 penalty kicks taken during regular game time, as opposed to part of penalty shootouts, indicates an advantage for the home team. It is currently unclear why analyses of penalty shootouts and penalty kicks during game time differ.

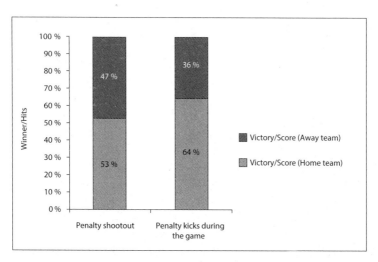

Figure 2. Comparison of a possible home field advantage during penalty shootouts in the DFB Cup games (1986-2006), and during National League games in Britain (based on data in the result section of Kocher et al., 2008, and Nevill et al., 1996).

REFERENCES

Kocher M. G., Lenz M. V., & Sutter M. (2008). Performance under pressure — The case of penalty shootouts in football. In Andersson P., Ayton P. & Schmidt C. (eds.) *Myths and Facts About Football: The Economics and Psychology of the World's Greatest Sport* (S. 61-72). Newcastle: Cambridge Scholars Publishing.

Nevill, A. M., Newell, S. M., & Gale, S. (1996). Factors associated with home advantage in English and Scottish soccer matches. Journal of Sports Sciences, 14(2), 181-186.

3

Does the team that scored the last goal during the match have a higher chance of winning the penalty shootout?

In the quarter-final of the FIFA World Cup 2014, Brazil hosted and played against the secret favorite team, Chile. The game was eventually decided on penalty kicks. In the 18th minute, David Luiz was able to score the opener with a left kick after Thiago Silva's assist. Even though Alexis Sánchez was able to equalize with a right kick after an assist from Eduardo Vargas 14 minutes later, the host team won the final penalty shootout because Chile missed three penalty kicks. The other quarter-final between Costa Rica and Greece was similar. Greek center back Sokratis Papastathopoulos scored the equalizing goal in stoppage time after Bryan Ruiz had scored the game's first goal early during the second half. However, Greece lost the quarter-final on penalty kicks, because Theofanis Gekas was not able to convert his penalty kick.

Despite the two opposing examples, there is the assumption that the team scoring the last goal, regardless of whether it happens in extra or regular game time, is more likely to win a penalty shootout. To test this theory, sports scientists have analyzed 407 games that were decided on penalty kicks and took place during the FIFA World Cups, FIFA European Championships, Africa Cups, Copa Americas, European Cups, and DFB Cups. The outcome of the decisive penalty shootout was noted, along with the team that scored last in regular or extra game time, among other variables. Analyses showed that the team that scored the last during game time won the following penalty shootout in 57% of all cases. Thus, scoring the (late) equalizer may result in a small psychological advantage, meaning that it may have had a positive effect on the self-efficacy of some players, possibly even the whole team. Additionally, the chance to leave the field as a winner after the penalty shootout may also increase.

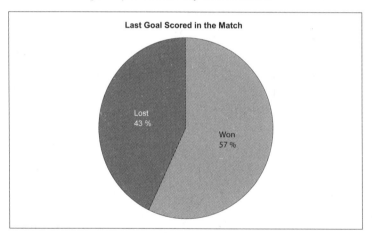

Figure 3. The likelihood of winning a penalty shootout for the team that scored the last goal vs. the team that conceded the last goal.

REFERENCES

Froese, G., & Plessner, H. (2010). In G. Amersberger, et al., Schriften der dvs, Band 201. Hamburg: Czwalina.

4

Are English penalty takers worse than their German counterparts?

Between 1990 and 2014, the English national team was involved in seven penalty shootouts in European Championships and FIFA World Cups. However, after losing six times, people's expectations for the FIFA World Cup in France were not too high. According to a survey in the *Times* in 2010, the largest concern in England was that the English national team would fail during a penalty shootout. Gareth Southgate got to the heart of it, stating that "the one thing people remember about me is: he can't score any penalties." Southgate was the only one who failed to score in the semi-finals of the FIFA World Cup against Germany, after England won their only penalty shootout in the quarter-final against Spain.

Is there scientific evidence to verify that English players miss penalty kicks more often than soccer players from different countries? It can be said that English players convert "only" about

68% of their penalty kicks at FIFA European Championships and World Cups, which is 7% less than the average. Only the Dutch have performed slightly worse (67%). When looking at penalty kick attempts, for which the opposing goalkeeper anticipated the kick direction correctly (no matter whether or not he was able to save the ball), English players come last.

In an attempt to scrutinize why some national teams perform worse than others, scientists have analyzed many penalty kicks during shootouts in huge tournaments, with a focus on team status and team performance. Team status means the standing in the world that players had at the time of a penalty shootout (i.e., how many international titles they have won with their team). The more successful players surprisingly took less of their time preparing for penalty kicks and were less successful than players of countries with lower team status. With a higher public status and seemingly more to lose than just a game, players from England and Spain have scored worse in penalty shootouts, perhaps because of worse self-regulation strategies.

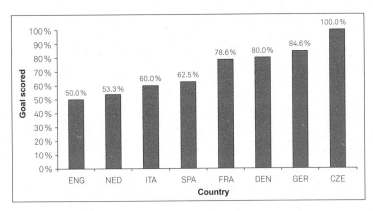

Figure 4. Countries and their goal success percentage when the goalie has moved in the right direction.

REFERENCES

Jordet, G. (2009). Why do English players fail in soccer penalty shootouts? A study of team status, self-regulation, and choking under pressure. Journal of Sports Sciences, 27, 97-10.

Should the player who was fouled in the box take the resulting penalty kick?

In spring 2012, the newspaper headlines read, "Loser of this season's top game, Arjen Robben: I am really sorry." Bayern Munich's Arjen Robben had missed the penalty kick against BVB that would have equalized the game. Franz Beckenbauer then stated: "With me as coach, Robben would not have taken the penalty kick himself. It is a soccer law that the player who was fouled should not take the penalty kick. Perhaps this law has been changed or has not yet arrived in the Netherlands?" Is it true that the person taking the kick is statistically relevant?

Today we know that the probability of scoring a penalty kick is 75% in the German Bundesliga. This percentage was determined after analyzing 3,768 penalty shots in the Bundesliga between 1963 and 2007. In talk shows or on the field, it is often said that the player who was fouled should not take the penalty kick himself. And there are many reasons for this assumption, such as "he is injured a bit," "he is still agitated because he was fouled;" or "there is a designated penalty taker on the team." Luckily, this assumption can be tested, as many data bank analyses have revealed. For example, all penalty kicks between 1993 and 2005 in the first Bundesliga were analyzed along with how they came about. (The analysis included 835 penalty shots from 229 different players from 30 different clubs.) Scientists examined which player was fouled, which of the players took the penalty kick, and whether he scored. The results revealed that there were no significant differences in likelihood of scoring between players who were fouled (72%) and other players (74%). This difference can be neglected from a statistical and practical perspective, as standard deviations must be considered.

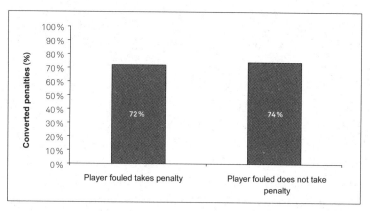

Figure 5. According to scientific findings, it does not matter who takes the penalty kick. The difference is negligible.

REFERENCES

Kuss, O., Kluttig, A., & Stoll, O. (2007). "The fouled player should not take the penalty himself": An empirical investigation of an old German football myth. Journal of Sports Sciences, 25, 963-967.

Bornkamp, B., Fritsch, A., Kuss, O., & Ickstadt, K. (2008). Penalty specialists among goalkeepers: A nonparametric Bayesian analysis of 44 years of German Bundesliga. In B. Schipp, & W. Krämer (Eds.), Statistical inference, econometric analysis and matrix algebra (pp. 63-67). Heidelberg: Springer.

6

What is the probability of two penalty kicks given to the same team in one match?

There were exciting matches with many penalty kicks in the 1965 Bundesliga matchday. Borussia Dortmund won 5-4 away against Borussia Mönchengladbach in Bökelberg stadium. In this match, believe it or not, the former record in the Bundesliga was beaten with five penalty kicks. Lothar Emmerich scored twice for the away team, and Milder and Netzer scored for the home team. Only Tilkowski missed in minute 78, which would have led to a tie for Gladbach. Is this number of penalty kicks usual?

Referees are supposed to perceive every game situation independently from game context and evaluate according to the set rules. Decisions on whether to whistle for a foul in the penalty box to be sanctioned with a penalty kick should not depend on whether a penalty kick was already given to the team. However, referees do sometimes make their decisions within the context of the game.

Studies demonstrate that, for example, the same foul situation can be evaluated completely differently (e.g., there is either a foul and a penalty kick, or no foul and no penalty kick), depending on whether the team has already had a penalty. In that case, a second penalty kick was practically never given. If the opposing team has already been given a penalty kick, the frequency of given penalty kicks increased (see figure).

Does the referee have a problem with giving two penalty kicks to a team in one game? The answer is yes, though the reason is still unclear. In line with game management, referees may make decisions which might be reasonable and conducive for soccer within the context of the game or competition. The term *game management* means that referees must be able to feel the game in order to control it smoothly and impartially.

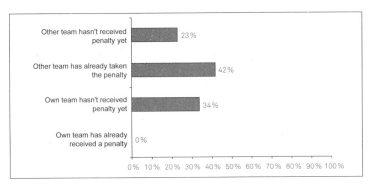

Figure 6. In an experimental study by Plessner & Betsch (2001), it was demonstrated that the probability of two penalty kicks for one team approaches zero. However, the probability increases as soon as the other team has already been given a penalty kick.

REFERENCES

Plessner, H., & Betsch, T. (2001). Sequential Effects in important Referee Decisions. Journal of Sport & Exercise Psychology, 23, 254–339.

Should the penalty taker wear a red jersey?

The color of the jersey has often been discussed in the media and at the regulars' table. In the UEFA European League 2014/15 final, Sevilla FC and SL Benfica played against each other. Benfica was not able to end their final's curse and lost the eighth international final match in a row. The final score was 4-2 after the penalty shootout. Could this be due to the color of the team's jersey? At the time, Sevilla was playing in white jerseys and Benfica in red jerseys.

There are a variety of study results indicating that the jersey color can have various meanings in many sports games. It was pointed out that in different sports, such as wrestling, boxing, and taekwondo, athletes in red clothing won more often than athletes in clothing of a another color. In reference to team sports, there are also similar findings stating that wearing a red jersey provides a competitive advantage. However, when looking at penalty kicks, there are contradictory results. Some studies suggest that goalkeepers, as well as penalty takers, can benefit from their red jerseys. For example, if the goalkeeper wears a red jersey, there are fewer successful penalty kicks because the color potentially influences the scorer negatively. However, if the scorer wears the red jersey, goalkeepers are less likely to evaluate their chances of saving the penalty kick. However, other studies were not able to confirm these results, so the situation remains slightly unclear. In some situations, wearing a red jersey does seem to have an effect, but this is not always the case. The problem is that it currently cannot be stated when, and for whom, a red jersey might be useful. Since there are no indications whatsoever that a red jersey has a negative influence on the person wearing it, wearing a red jersey should be encouraged. Consequently Benfica was not able to use the excuse of the jersey color after the game.

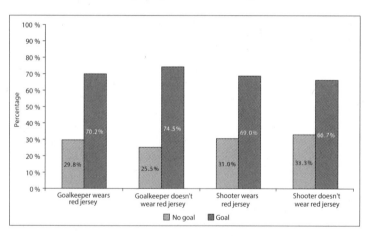

Figure 7. The relation of hits and misses if a penalty taker or goalkeeper wears a red jersey or a jersey of a different color.

REFERENCES

Hill, R.A., & Barton R.A. (2005). Red enhances human performance in contests. Nature, 435, 293.

Greenlees, I., Eynon, M., & Thelwell, R. (2013). Color of soccer goalkeepers' uniforms influences the outcome of penalty kicks. Perceptual & Motor Skills, 117, 1-10.

Greenlees, I., Leyland, A., Thelwell, R., & Filby, W. (2008). Soccer penalty takers' uniform color and pre-penalty kick gaze affect the impressions formed by opposing goalkeepers. Journal of Sport Sciences, 26, 569-576.

Noël, B., Furley, P., Hüttermann, S., Nopp, S., Vogelbein, M., & Memmert, D. (2014). Einflussfaktoren auf Erfolg und Misserfolg beim Elfmeterschießen. Eine empiriegeleitete retrospektive Analyse der Europa- und Weltmeisterschaften von 1982 bis 2012. Zeitschrift für Sportpsychologie, 21, 51-62.

The Penalty Taker

Should the penalty taker be promotion oriented?

We can frequently see that coaches allow the captain or another good player to carry out the penalty kick. These players are most often forwards or midfielders—for example, Bayern Munich's Thomas Müller or Robert Lewandowski. For FC Barcelona, it is Lionel Messi, and for Real Madrid, Cristiano Ronaldo. Surprisingly, there are few defenders or even goalkeepers who are asked to carry out a penalty kick. However, there are also goalkeepers who have a much better success rate than many forwards and midfielders. Hans Jörg Butt, for example, has converted 26 penalty kicks (three of them in the Champions League) during his time at Hamburger SV, Bayer 04 Leverkusen, and FC Bayern Munich. Therefore, he is the best penalty taker among goalkeepers in the history of the German Bundesliga, with a high success rate of 81.82%. Furthermore, he is definitely better than the average of in the German Bundesliga (75%).

We know from sports psychology that offensive players are mostly promotion oriented, and defensive players, as well as goalkeepers, are prevention oriented. Current motivation theories illustrate why this can be important for performance in penalty kicking.

Motivation theories distinguish two forms of self-regulation when striving for a desired result. These are the promotion–focus (i.e., when the focus relies on fulfillment and hope) and the prevention–focus (i.e., the focus relies on security and obligation). They describe a performance advantage if a person is in a situation, which corresponds with preferred focus ("Regulatory Fit"). This means that the combination of the specific requirements of a task and the basic orientation of soccer players has an impact on the respective performance. Research showed that the success rate of penalty takers is higher when they were instructed in some way beforehand, which corresponds with their basic motivational orientation, compared to cases in which they were not instructed at all. Particularly more penalty kicks were converted when dutiful players were given direct instructions. This shows that the fit between an athlete's personality and the current situation and environmental requirements have a decisive role on success in penalty kicking.

Coaches improve a team's chances of winning a penalty shootout if they select players who have a distinct obligation attitude and convey that it is their duty to convert the penalty kick. Therefore, it seems advisable to also summon defenders or even goalkeepers.

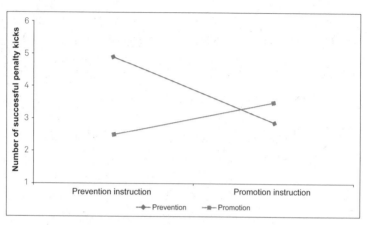

Figure 8. In a situation in which a dutiful player feels obligated to score (i.e., it is their duty), the probability of success is highest.

REFERENCES

Plessner, H., Unkelbach, C., Memmert, D., Baltes, A., & Kolb, A. (2009). Regulatory Fit as a Determinant of Sport Performance. Psychology of Sport & Exercise, 10, 108–115.

Should the penalty taker be left-footed?

Ricardo Rodriguez is known as one of the best penalty takers in the Bundesliga and in Europe. Out of 15 penalty kicks taken in his active career, he converted 13, which resulted in an unbelievable success rate of 87%. His only miss in the Bundesliga was against Bayer Leverkusen and goalkeeper Bernd Leno, when Wolfsburg still won 3-1. He was also unable to score his penalty kick attempt during the 90th minute of the UEFA European Championships qualification match (2015) against San Marino's goalkeeper, Aldo Simoncini. However, it was already 4-0 for Switzerland, so it did not come as a shock. One last piece of information is that Ricardo Rodriguez is left-footed. Could this have an influence on penalty kick performance?

In sports science, the trend is relatively clear. A strategic advantage is assumed for left-handed and left-footed players, not only because there are fewer of them in general, but also because there are fewer in professional sports. This means most players are simply not used to playing against players with a strong left arm or foot. In soccer, players like Arjen Robben, Diego Maradona, and Lionel Messi directly come to mind because they have all shot and scored penalty kicks frequently. But do players with a strong left foot really have an advantage in penalty shootout situations?

Using video footage, McMorris and Colenso (1996) tested the anticipation ability of soccer players and were able to demonstrate that the kick direction of left-footed players is less predictable than the kick direction of right-footed penalty takers. Other researchers hypothesized that this is related to the fact that goalkeepers are simply less often confronted with left-footed players and, therefore, have less experience with such penalty takers. However, and this is important, the analyses of success rates of left- and right-footed players lead to contradictory results. For instance, at the FIFA World Cup and the FIFA European Championship, there are actually no results that point to left-footed penalty takers scoring more than right-footed penalty takers. However, left-footed players kicked as often to the right side as to the left, whereas right-footed players kicked to the left side more frequently (from their point of view). To summarize, goalkeepers seem to have more problems with opponents kicking with the left foot. This, however, does not seem to increase the chances of left-footed players scoring.

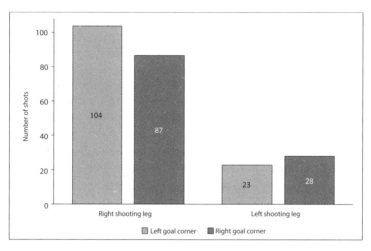

Figure 9: Distribution according to shooting leg for kicks to the right or left as seen from the player's position.

REFERENCES

Baumann, F., Friehe, T., & Wedow, M. (2011). General ability and specialization: Evidence from penalty kicks in soccer. Journal of Sports Economics, 12, 81-105.

McMorris, T., & Colenso, S. (1996). Anticipation of professional soccer goalkeepers when facing right- and left-footed penalty kicks. Perceptual and Motor Skills, 82, 931-934.

Noël, B., Furley, P., Hüttermann, S., Nopp, S., Vogelbein, M., & Memmert, D. (2014). Einflussfaktoren auf Erfolg und Misserfolg beim Elfmeterschießen. Eine empiriegeleitete retrospektive Analyse der Europa- und Weltmeisterschaften von 1982 bis 2012. Zeitschrift für Sportpsychologie, 21, 51-62.

Should the penalty taker use pre-performance routines?

In the quarter-final of the 2016 UEFA European Championship, Italian forward Simone Zaza received a lot of attention because of his penalty kick attempt. He ran up awkwardly and missed his penalty kick. It is notable that he used the same way to run up at subsequent penalty kicks and, therefore, it seems possible this is an example of a performance routine (https://www.youtube.com/watch?v=AKILVnECGBI). The best-known pre-performance routine in soccer looks like this: putting down the ball, taking big steps backwards, and resting with legs apart and hands on hips. This is a well-known routine for Cristiano Ronaldo. Even though he does this before a free kick rather than a penalty kick, the reasoning is probably transferable to penalty kicks. A lot of players use pre-performance routines and rituals to prepare for a penalty kick, though the majority of these cannot be easily detected (i.e., taking a deep breath). But do pre-performance routines have an effect, and is developing a routine worth it?

The goal with using a pre-performance routine is to prepare in exactly the right way using the right amount of preparation time to increase the likelihood of success. Regarding pre-performance routines, different studies illustrated that a player should take enough preparation time before a penalty kick. Furthermore, using pre-performance routines can prevent athletes from becoming easily distracted or not being in the right emotional condition to perform well. However, there is not much research on pre-performance routines in penalty kicking. In other sports, such as basketball or rugby, pre-performance routines aren't rare, and there are more research results.

However, these are partly contradictory. Some studies indicate that pre-performance routines in different sports can lead to an improvement in performance. In water polo (at least in some way comparable to the penalty kick in soccer), it was pointed out that players improve their penalty throws when they have trained pre-performance routines over an extended period of time. However, an analysis of 572 tries in which the ball must be shot between the crossbars of the goal at the Rugby World Cup led to different results. The more and less successful players cannot be distinguished based on how they prepare and make use of pre-performance routines (duration, rhythm, consistency). It is not known which results can be transferred to penalty kicking in soccer. Until then, however, it can simply be stated that players probably cannot do anything wrong when using pre-performance routines. That is, there is no need to assume that performance suffers from specific preparation. Whether the time used to establish pre-performance routines can be used differently, is another story.

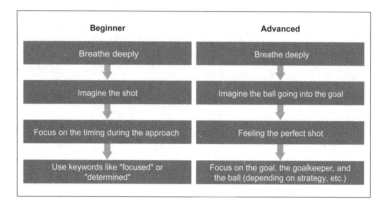

Figure 10. Two examples of behavior routines before a penalty kick. Beginners should concentrate on the kicking attempt. Advanced players can depend on an automated process and rely on their feelings.

REFERENCES

Jackson, R. C. (2003). Pre-performance routine consistency: temporal analysis of goal kicking in the Rugby Union World Cup. *Journal of Sport Sciences, 21,* 803-814.

Jackson, R. C., & Baker, J. S. (2001). Routines, Rituals, and Rugby: Case of a World Class Goal Kicker. *Sport Psychologist, 15,* 48-65.

Marlow, C., Bull, S. J., Heath, B. & Shambrook, C. J. (1998). The use of a single case design to investigate the effect of a pre-performance routine on the water polo penalty shot. *Journal of Science and Medicine in Sport, 1,* 143-155.

Is a goalkeeper's behavior predictable?

Portugal and England met in the FIFA European Championships 2004 semi-final, and the team qualifying for the next round was decided by penalty kicks. The Portuguese goalkeeper, Ricardo, became the penalty shootout hero because he not only saved England's last penalty kick, but afterwards also converted the decisive penalty kick, making it 8-7.

The Portuguese penalty takers kicked four shots in a row into the left corner (as seen from the penalty taker). England's goalkeeper David James chose the wrong corner against the first penalty taker. After that, he dived to the left corner twice in a row, but against the fourth penalty taker, James decided to use the right corner to defend. Did the choice of the kick direction and move direction occur randomly, or was the goalkeeper's behavior in any manner predictable? Is it possible to observe the goalkeeper and predict which corner he will likely dive to in order to save the next penalty kick?

From a scientific perspective, the behavior of the goalkeeper seems predictable in some situations. Broadly speaking, goalkeepers can choose from two strategic behaviors: They can either commit to one side early and speculate to a certain extent (depending on how long before the kick they decide for a corner) or try to react to a kick. Most goalkeepers choose the first option. They want to anticipate and commit early. However, goalkeepers do not always rely on their anticipation performance or knowledge on preferences of the penalty taker when choosing a corner. They also consider what the previous penalty takers did. Of course, this often happens intuitively, or without the goalkeeper being aware of it. This is a natural behavior but can sometime cause problems, comparable to a coin toss. When it has landed on the head side several times in a row, someone might assume that it is more likely to land on the tail side the next time. However, this is not the case since chances are still at 50%.

Something similar can be observed when three successive penalty takers of a team have kicked into the same corner. The expectation that the next penalty taker will kick into the other corner wrongly increases. This increases the probability of the goalkeeper to decide for the other corner in those situations. The idea of a penalty taker eventually having to kick to the other side is undoubtedly understandable, but also dangerous. However, penalty takers rarely make use of those tendencies of the goalkeeper. This indicates that penalty takers and coaches are not aware of all their options. The possibility to design team strategies (which penalty taker kicks to the left/right side) seems to be a possibility to increase a team's chances to win.

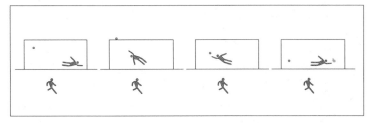

Figure 11: Four consecutive kicks by Portuguese players against the English goalkeeper during the penalty shootout in the semi-final of the 2004 FIFA European Championship. The Portuguese players are presented in red, the English goalkeeper in blue; the green circle represents the ball. All four kicks were kicked to the left goal side. The goalkeeper committed to the right side after three consecutive kicks to the left (from Misirlisoy & Haggard, 2014).

REFERENCES

Braun, S., & Schmidt, U. (2015). The gambler's fallacy in penalty shootouts. *Current Biology, 25,* R597-R598.

Kuhn, W. (1988). Penalty-kick strategies for penalty takers and goalkeepers. In A. L. T. Reilly, K. Davids & W. J. Murphy (Eds.), *Science and football* (S. 489-492). London: E & FN Spon.

Misirlisoy, E., & Haggard, P. (2014). Asymmetric predictability and cognitive competition in football penalty shootouts. *Current Biology, 24,* 1918-1922.

Misirlisoy, E., & Haggard, P. (2014). Reply to Braun and Schmidt. *Cognitive Psychology, 25,* R599.

12

Does the approach angle matter in penalty kicking?

Ronaldinho, the Brazilian World Soccer Player of 2004 and 2005, had a diagonal run-up during penalty shootouts. Before approaching the ball, he was located only slightly diagonally toward the ball; however, he modified his run-up angle with one or two steps to the side so that he had a more oblique run-up angle than other penalty takers. During his career, he missed 16 penalty kicks and converted 58. His rate is slightly above the average 78%. In 2002, he became World Champion with Brazil, and in 2005/06, he won the Spanish Championship, the Super Cup, and became Champions League Winner with FC Barcelona. Ronaldinho was occasionally known as an "odd character" because he wore the back number 80 because he was born in 1980.

The scientific answer to the question of whether the run-up angle matters is yes, because the run-up angle counts as the early cues that can inform the goalkeeper where the penalty taker will kick. Scientists were able to demonstrate that goalkeepers are influenced by the run-up angle. Their anticipation of imminent penalty kicks was best for a mid-run-up angle (20 and 30 degrees) and worst when the run-up angle was extremely straight or lopsided (0 or 40 degrees). On the one hand, focusing on the run-up angle of the penalty taker or other early cues provides a time advantage which allows the goalkeeper to react to the plan of the penalty taker. But on the other hand, it gives the penalty taker time to change his mind or even use deceptive movement. This means that although the run-up angle provides knowledge about the plans of the penalty taker, it is a relatively unreliable source of information for the goalkeeper.

Goalkeepers who decide to commit to one side earlier (also based on information about the run-up angle of the penalty taker) benefit when they decide on the right side (before they can reach a ball; they wouldn't be able to reach when starting to move later), but they also easily fall for deceptions (e.g., a consciously chosen run-up angle). Therefore, it is not surprising that better goalkeepers wait longer before starting a final movement, because that way they will be sure enough of which direction they must defend. Better goalkeepers are often more agile and can therefore wait longer in order to gain more information. However, they do seem to be aware of the run-up angle not being a reliable indicator, unless combined with other sources of information, allowing them to interpret the intentions of the penalty taker. This can either be information the goalkeeper takes from other aspects of the penalty taker's movements, or scouting information on the usual procedure of a penalty taker.

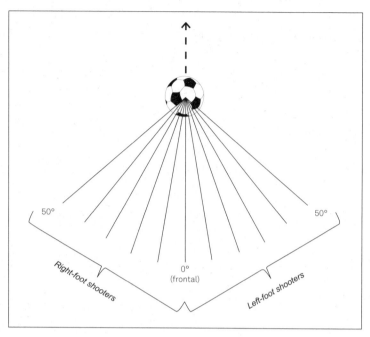

Figure 12. Overview of different run-up angles of penalty takers with the left and right foot.

REFERENCES

Savelsbergh G. J. P., van der Kamp, J., Williams, A. M., & Ward, P. (2005). Anticipation and visual search behaviour in expert soccer goalkeepers. Ergonomics, 48, 1686-1697.

Loffing, F., & Hagemann, N. (2014). Zum Einfluss des Anlaufwinkels und der Füßigkeit des Schützen auf die Antizipation von Elfmeterschüssen. Zeitschrift für Sportpsychologie, 21, 63-73.

13

Should the penalty taker decide on target direction before running up?

We all know how Thomas Müller carries out penalty kicks. He has practiced it innumerable times during training sessions. He has a rehearsed run-up, during which he continuously fixes on the goalkeeper and does not even look at the ball when kicking. His success rate was 83% in the Bundesliga 2013/14 and 2014/15 seasons, which is appreciably higher than the average in the German professional soccer league. During the last season, the rate decreased and currently only lies at 50%. Goalkeepers have most likely started to prepare for his strategy.

Eden Hazard from Real Madrid uses a similar kicking strategy as Thomas Müller, with an even higher success rate. It was at 90% in 2013/14 and 2014/15. Should the penalty taker react to the goalkeeper's movements like Hazard or Müller? Or should he decide on a target direction before running up?

According to sports science, there are two strategic approaches distinguished in penalty kicking. These are known as the keeper dependent strategy and the keeper independent strategy. In the keeper dependent strategy, the penalty taker, for example Thomas Müller, looks at the goalkeeper. This means that he waits for a reaction from the goalkeeper in order to kick to the open goal side. In keeper independent strategy, penalty takers determine where they want to kick before the run-up and try to not be distracted by the goalkeeper.

Penalty takers are often advised not to consider the goalkeeper's movements because it can lead to various problems. What does a penalty taker do when, for example, he gets closer to the ball, and the goalkeeper does not move? Furthermore, penalty takers who focus on the goalkeeper tend to kick more in the goalkeeper's direction as a consequence of their gaze. However, in an analysis of all penalty shootouts at UEFA European Championships and FIFA World Cups from 1984-2012, no differences between both strategies could be found with regard to their effectiveness. Both strategies lead to a similar success rate. However, it was noticeable that penalty takers rarely tried to employ keeper dependent strategy. This was potentially because it seems more difficult to practice. To sum up, there is probably no best way to strategically approach a penalty kick, at least not in general.

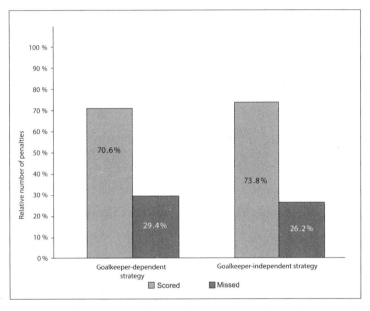

Figure 13. Relative number of successful penalty kicks depending on penalty kick strategy used at FIFA World Cups and UEFA European Championships between 1984 and 2012 (Noël et al., 2015).

REFERENCES

Noël, B., Furley, P., van der Kamp, J., Dicks, M., & Memmert, D. (2015). The development of a method for identifying penalty kick strategies in association football. *Journal of Sport Sciences*, 33, 1-10.

Noël, B., & van der Kamp, J. (2006). Gaze behaviour during the soccer penalty kick: An investigation of the effects of strategy and anxiety. *International Journal of Sport Psychology*, 43, 326-345.

Should the penalty kicker take his time during the kicking process?

An exciting question: How much time should a penalty kicker take after the referee blows the whistle before he kicks the ball? In February 2013, the fans at the HDI Arena were witnesses of a very strange, maybe even the longest, penalty kick in history. Hannover 96 met Makhachkala in the European League game. Hannover player Christian Schulz committed a foul against Samuel Eto'o—the best-paid player on the planet at that time (approx. 20 million Euros). Eto'o stepped up to take, arguably, the most arrogant penalty kick in soccer history. He took a run-up of 13 meters! And he did not cover that distance quickly, instead walking in the direction of the ball so slowly that the Hannover players complained to the referee. He finally kicked the ball after 14 little steps. This run-up lasted for—believe it or not— 12 seconds. The TV reporter shouted into the microphone: "He steps up to the point, he strides like a king. Super arrogant! Super arrogant!" Ron-Robert Zieler, the Hannover goalkeeper, saved the ball.

From a scientific point of view, it can be assumed that penalty takers can take too little time when it comes to penalty kicks. On the other hand, they can also perform badly when it takes too long for them to start the penalty kick. A group of scientists analyzed all penalty kicks at FIFA World Cups, UEFA European Championships, and in UEFA Champions League competitions and came to the conclusion that penalty takers are more often successful when they take more time to start with the run-up after the referee whistles.

One experiment showed that a quick penalty kick procedure is considered hasty and insecure behavior by the goalkeeper. From a player's perspective, this kind of behavior can be explained as them wanting the unpleasant situation to be over and done with as soon as possible. This can be referred to as "flight behavior." Goalkeepers estimate a higher chance of saving the ball in those situations, causing them to take more time to start a defensive action. However, there is also a connection between an excessively long wait for the referee's signal and the following penalty taker's probability of success. Those results are based on the analysis of the penalty shootouts mentioned previously in arguably the most important competitions. However, you will not automatically take better penalty kicks if you take the right amount of time. The waiting period is an expression of various influencing factors on the success of penalty kicks, such as self-confidence. Therefore, it seems necessary to choose a deeper approach (something that improves penalty takers' self-confidence) in order to become a successful penalty taker. Consequently, the waiting period and body language will automatically change in a penalty kick situation.

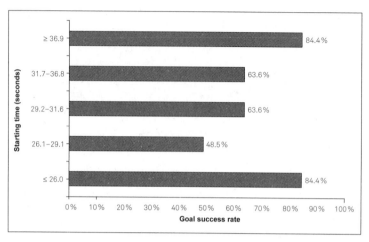

Image 14. The connection between the time a penalty kicker takes for his run-up and the performance at penalty shootouts (Jordet et al., 2009).

REFERENCES

Furley, P., Dicks, M., Stendtke, F., & Memmert, D. (2012). "Get it out the way. The wait's killing me." Hastening and hiding during soccer penalty kicks. *Psychology of Sport and Exercise, 13,* 454-465.

Jordet, G., Hartman, E., & Sigmunstad, E. (2009). Temporal links to performing under pressure in international soccer penalty shootouts. *Psychology of Sport and Exercise, 10,* 621-627.

Is it possible, as a penalty taker, to completely ignore the goalkeeper?

In reference to missing the decisive penalty kick during the 1994 FIFA World Cup final between Brazil and Italy, Roberto Baggio, the former Italian world-class striker and national player, says, "This has followed me for years. It is the worst moment of my career. I still dream about it. If I could erase a moment, this would be the moment." The quote (published in his autobiography in 2001) demonstrates just how much pressure there is on the penalty taker when in an important penalty kick situation. Is it possible to ignore the goalkeeper and only concentrate on the target in the stressful situation of a penalty kick, in a case where the goalkeeper virtually owns the goal and therefore the situation and outcome?

Based on a field experiment with 10 middle-class penalty takers, goalkeepers are hard to ignore. In the experiment, penalty takers were asked to kick to one of the target zones; one zone was in the right and the other in the left top corner of the goal. In some cases, a goalkeeper was in the goal, and sometimes not. Penalty takers were asked to decide on a target zone before the actual attempt, meaning that ignoring the goalkeeper was theoretically possible. If they were able to hit the target zone, the goalkeeper only had a small chance to hold the ball. Nevertheless, it was observed that the goalkeeper's presence influenced the penalty taker. Kicks were less accurate, meaning that they were more toward the middle of the goal when a goalkeeper was positioned in the goal. The effect was even stronger when goalkeepers knew which direction the penalty takers would shoot.

This is generally interpreted as distracting and even intimidating stimuli in the environment (here done by the goalkeeper), disturbing and interrupting the normal movement process in some way. They are automatically taken into consideration, and so kicks, throws, and so on end closer to the distraction-causing stimulus as a consequence. If kicks tend more toward the center of the goal when the goalkeeper is in the goal, it can be seen as an indication that the goalkeeper cannot be easily ignored. In such an experiment, there is not much in it for a penalty taker, and the goalkeepers seem less threatened and have therefore been largely passive. Based on other studies, it can also be said that goalkeepers who move receive even more unwanted attention. It is obviously in the interest of the penalty taker to place the ball farther away from the goalkeeper. Therefore, scorers who decide to employ the keeper independent strategy should not only train their kicking movement, but also their gaze behavior in order to be able to hit accurately and not give the goalkeeper any chance to save the ball.

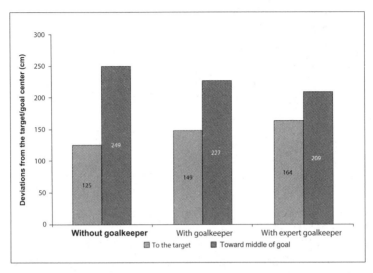

Figure 15. Mean for distances (cm) between the goal center and the place where the ball crossed the goal line (Navarro et al., 2013).

REFERENCES

Baggio, R. (2005). *Una porta nel cielo.* Villasanta: Limina.

Navarro, M., van der Kamp, J., Ranvaud, R. & Savelsbergh, G. J. P. (2013). The mere presence of a goalkeeper affects the accuracy of penalty kicks. *Journal of Sport Sciences, 31,* 921-929.

16

Should the penalty taker aim for a target just under the cross bar?

The most spectacular penalty kicks are when the ball hits the net just below the bar. They are technically very difficult, but beautiful. İlkay Gündoğan was able to accomplish this for Borussia Dortmund in the 2015 German Cup semi-final against FC Bayern Munich. Frank Lampard has also scored in a similar way against FC Bayern Munich during the penalty shootout of the 2013 UEFA Super Cup final. Lampard kicked the ball into the upper right corner to make it 5-5. However, this goal did not help them in the end. Dramatically, the Bavarian team was able to defeat their opponent in penalty kicks and win the European Super Cup for the first time. During game time, Chelsea London led two times, but Bayern Munich was able to score two equalizers. During the penalty shootout, every penalty taker scored until it was 7-6. After that, Manuel Neuer saved the last penalty kick by Lukaku (Chelsea).

Kicks to the upper region of the goal are seen as playing it safe. This might be the case because goalkeepers generally have no chance of saving a ball that is kicked high in the upper third. There is not enough time for the goalkeeper to reach such a kick. In various studies using different analyzed time frames, it was also confirmed that no single kick in the upper third of the goal was saved. But does this mean that everyone should aim for the upper goal region? Well, it is more complicated than that.

In our analysis of 34 penalty shootouts at big international tournaments, we were able to indicate that no penalty shot kicked to the upper third of the goal was saved. However, roughly every fourth penalty kick that was aimed high was kicked too high, and either hit the crossbar or went over it. This is about the same rate of missed penalty kicks as in low attempts. The thing that effectively changes is the way that penalty kicks are missed. That is, goalkeepers do not save the shot, but rather the goal is more often completely missed. So, if one wants to be independent of the goalkeeper and able to kick the ball very accurately, the decision to aim for the upper goal area is logical. It seems that not only the own kicking movement, but also every other aspect of someone's behavior can lead to a successful penalty kick, but shooting in the upper third should be trained intensely. However, if someone wants to employ a keeper dependent strategy or does not want to risk missing the goal, he should not aim for the upper part of the goal. If the goalkeeper chooses the wrong side of the goal, kicking accuracy does not matter. The ball crosses the goal line, and the goalkeeper has no chance to reach it because he is already moving in the opposite direction.

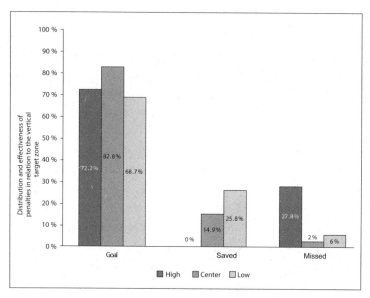

Figure 16. Distribution and effectiveness of penalty kicks as related to the vertical goal zone (high, center, low) (from Noël et al. 2014).

REFERENCES

Bar-Eli, M., & Azar, O. H. (2009). Penalty kicks in soccer: An empirical analysis of shooting strategies and goalkeepers' preferences. *Soccer and Society*, 10, 183-191.

Bar-Eli, M. Azar, O. H., & Lurie, Y. (2009). (Ir) rationality in action: Do soccer players and goalkeepers fail to learn how to best perform during a penalty kick? In M. Raab, J. G. Johnson & H. R. Reekers (Eds.), Progress in brain research (Vol. 174, S. 97-108). Amsterdam: Elsevier B.V.

Noël, B., Furley, P., Hüttermann, S., Nopp, S., Vogelbein, M., & Memmert, D. (2014). Einflussfaktoren auf Erfolg und

Misserfolg beim Elfmeterschießen. Eine empiriegeleitete retrospektive Analyse der Europa- und Weltmeisterschaften von 1982 bis 2012. *Zeitschrift für Sportpsychologie,* 21, 51-62.

17

Should the penalty taker focus on the target area during the kicking process?

In order to answer this question, several aspects must be considered. First of all, it is dependent on the strategy that the scorer uses. If he wants to employ a keeper dependent strategy, he is simply not able to focus on the target area because he often does not know until very late during the run-up where he wants to kick. It is a different story if the penalty taker has decided where and how he wants to kick before his run-up. In this case, focusing on the target area makes sense.

Studies on gaze behavior during penalty kicks and different sport game situations, for example, the basketball free throw or the putt in golf, show that the accuracy of a kick or throw increases and improves performance if one looks extensively toward the direction of the target while aiming. This phenomenon is called "Quiet Eye" in the literature. Additional training forms have been developed with aims to instruct athletes to focus on targets. However, in some respects the penalty kick situation is more complex than free throws in basketball games. In penalty kicking, there are two different targets: to hit the ball correctly and to hit the goal with the ball.

According to the definition of "Quiet Eye," gaze should be directed to the target shortly before the beginning of a movement. During the penalty kick and run-up, it is hard to determine when one phase is ending (before which you should look at the ball) and when the other phase is beginning (before which you should look toward the goal). Another decisive difference between a basketball free throw and a penalty kick is that in penalty kicking, another opponent, namely the goalkeeper, can interfere, whereas during a free throw, you can look as long as needed toward the basket without risking interference. You must also keep in mind that the goalkeeper gets information on the penalty taker's intentions based on the kicker's gaze behavior. To summarize, it seems to make sense to focus on the target, if it is possible. However, it should be considered that there is more than one target to focus on. While on the one hand, it is important to look at the ball, on the other hand, for penalty takers who want to react to the goalkeeper's movements, it is essential to also look at the goalkeeper.

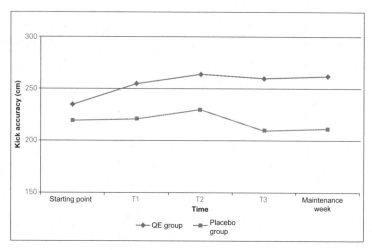

Figure 17. Kick accuracy for Quiet Eye and control groups before and after training, and in the (performance) preservation weeks (from Wood & Wilson, 2011).

REFERENCES

Harle, S. K., & Vickers, J. N. (2001). Training Quiet Eye Improves accuracy in the basketball free throw. *The Sport Psychologist,* 15, 289-305.

Noël, B., & van der Kamp, J. (2012). Gaze behaviour during the soccer penalty kick: An investigation of the effects of strategy and anxiety. *International Journal of Sport Psychology,* 43, 326–345.

Vickers, J. N. (2012). Neuroscience of the Quiet Eye in golf putting. *International Journal of Golf Science,* 1, 2-9.

Wood, G., & Wilson, M. R. (2011). Quiet-eye training for soccer penalty kicks. *Cognitive Processing,* 12, 257-266.

Wood, G., & Wilson, M. R. (2012) Quiet-eye training, perceived control and performing under pressure. *Psychology of Sport & Exercise,* 13, 721-728.

18

Should the penalty taker avoid pointing the non-kicking foot in the shooting direction?

The dream of bringing back home the third FIFA World Cup title for the German Women national team was broken on June 30, 2015. In the semi-final against the US, Sylvia Neid's team were beaten after 90 minutes with an end result of 0-2. The tragic figure of the evening in Montreal was Germany's number 13 who initiated the loss with her missed penalty kick in the 60th minute, when the score was still 0-0. In the following game, the American women were able to defeat titleholder Japan easily, 5-2. As a right-footed player, Célia Šašić kicked to the left side and thereby positioned her non-kicking leg so that her toes pointed to the right corner. Was this an attempt to fool the American goalkeeper, Hope Solo?

Célia Šašić has always been a relatively good penalty taker whose non-kicking foot was not always pointed toward the actual kick direction. This makes it harder for the goalkeepers, who want to anticipate kick direction based on a penalty taker's movement, to jump to the correct goal side in time to reach the ball. However, and this is at least of theoretical importance, the direction in which the non-kicking leg points prior to the kick is a reliable indicator which can be used by goalkeepers who want to anticipate kick direction early. If a penalty taker aims for the left side, the toes of the non-kicking leg automatically point in the direction of the left goal corner. During kicks to the right side, the toes point to the right side of the goal. However, this does not mean that penalty takers should avoid pointing the non-kicking leg in the direction of the target.

Though this information gives the goalkeeper fairly more time to react (whether or not it is enough depends on the agility of the goalkeeper), this aspect of the kicking movement corresponds to a natural motion sequence which is trained over the years. Here, it makes more sense for the kick and gaze behavior of penalty takers to be trained in a way that allows penalty takers to kick as accurately as possible. In this case, a goalkeeper who has more information on the penalty taker's intentions has an increased chance of jumping toward the correct corner (in about 80% of the cases). If the kick is hard and placed well enough (the chance is higher if there are no artificial interruptions in the natural kicking movement), it does not make any difference in the end for the scorer. However, a goalkeeper is still advised to look at important aspects of the kick direction facing weaker penalty takers, such as the orientation of the non-kicking leg. It helps to focus on body language to identify the kick direction.

Collecting as much information as possible in order to increase the chance of saving a not well-placed kick seems to be a fairly promising approach. For penalty takers who want to employ a keeper dependent strategy, the direction of the non-kicking leg shortly before or during the kick is not important. A goalkeeper has already decided on a direction or remained in the middle of the goal. In this case, the information revealed by the orientation of the non-kicking leg is not helpful.

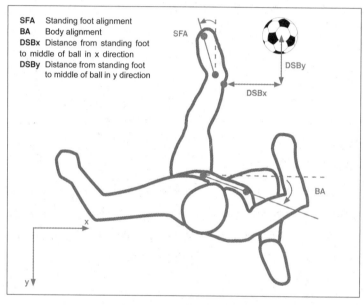

Figure 18. Measurements of kinematical variables for the placement of the non-kicking leg (from an overhead perspective). The angle counterclockwise is positive (SFO: orientation of the stable foot; PLO: orientation of the breast; DSBx: distance of the heel of the non-kicking leg to the ball middle in direction x; DSBy: distance of the heel of the non-kicking leg to the ball middle in direction y) (from Li et al. 2015).

REFERENCES

Lees, A., & Owens, L. (2011). Early visual cues associated with a directional place kick in soccer. *Sports Biomechanics,* 10, 125-134.

Li, Y., Alexander, M. J. L., Glazenbrook, M., & Leier, J. (2015). Prediction of kick direction from kinematics during the soccer penalty kick. *International Journal of Kinesiology & Sport Science,* 3, 1-7.

19

Does a team benefit from penalty takers celebrating a successful penalty kick attempt?

Do you remember the quarter-final between Uruguay and Ghana in the 2010 FIFA World Cup in South Africa? Ghana barely missed the semi-finals as the first African team in this historic game. The Black Stars took the lead in the first half thanks to Muntari's shot from about 30 meters, but the two-time World Champion equalized in minute 55. Forlan's free kick sailed into the far corner. In extra time, the Black Stars were the superior team and were awarded a penalty kick, but to the shock of the South African fans who were all supporting Ghana at this point, Gyan kicked the ball against the cross bar, giving away their victory. During the penalty shootout, Uruguay kept the upper hand. It is, however, the penalty kick by Appiah that comes to mind. He theatrically celebrated his converted penalty kick attempt to make it 3-3. After remaining in the penalty area for a long time, he clapped his hands above his head and tried to motivate the fans behind the goal to be more active. Directly after scoring, he also yelled loudly and hit his chest. Does such behavior have a positive effect after a successful penalty kick?

To answer this question, scientists at the University of Groningen analyzed every penalty shootout at the UEFA European Championship and the FIFA World Cup between 1972 and 2008. Altogether, there were 325 penalty kicks, out of which 75% were converted. Results indicate that post-goal celebrations seem to have a positive effect on the outcome of a penalty shootout of two equally strong teams. This means that subsequent penalty takers of the opposing team failed to score more often if the successful player of the other team visibly celebrated the goal. Indeed, one conclusion to draw from this is that players should celebrate a successful penalty kick to influence the following players. Whether or not less spontaneous cheering "on command" actually works has yet to be sufficiently tested. Nevertheless, you've got nothing to lose with a gesture of celebration.

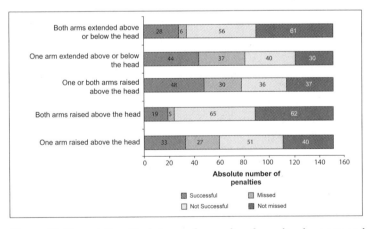

Figure 19. The relationship between the results of penalty shootouts and different forms of cheering after a converted penalty kick attempt (taken from Moll et al., 2010).

REFERENCES

Moll, T., Jordet, G., & Pepping, G. (2010). Emotional contagion in soccer penalty shootouts: Celebration of individual success is associated with ultimate team success. *Journal of Sport Sciences, 28*, 983-992.

The Goalkeeper

How can a goalkeeper improve his anticipation skills?

Goalkeeper coach Michael Rechner (TSG 1899 Hoffenheim) is known for his innovative and excellent goalkeeper training. He often tries to recreate actual situations during competitions to improve the anticipation abilities of his players as well as observation abilities and quick decision-making skills. Each of his training aspects is based on what is afforded goalkeepers during competitions. He has created a requirement profile based on game analyses, which he then applies on the training field. Technical and tactical key points are developed to then train them in game-relevant forms. Next to the specific techniques, tactical elements such as decision-making or game-relevant perception are learned in game-phase forms.

An important aspect of a goalkeeper's perception in penalty shootouts is his anticipation performance. A goalkeeper usually has too little time to react to a kick from the penalty mark, so needs to try to anticipate the penalty taker's behavior. Even though several studies point to cues with which a goalkeeper can predict the penalty taker's intention at an early stage (e.g., kick direction or penalty kick strategy), teaching this ability is more difficult than it would first appear. Theoretical knowledge on its own, for example, knowing how a player could act and which cues to pay attention to, cannot simply be transformed into a performance increase. If a goalkeeper is taught too much information, then his behavior and reaction slow down because he spends too much time considering what he should actually do. This is fatal in situations when a goalkeeper has very little time. How can we help a goalkeeper to improve his or her anticipation performance without overloading him or her with theoretical knowledge about the movement and behavior of the penalty taker?

Latest findings based on an experiment with 18 inexperienced goalkeepers fortify the impression that anticipation is probably best trained, directly on the field. Goalkeepers who were trained specifically (three players simultaneously approaching the ball, but only one of them running and carrying out the penalty kick, without the goalkeeper knowing which of them would be the penalty taker), improving their anticipation performance even more than those goalkeepers who participated in regular training which required them to defend a number of normal penalty kicks. Goalkeepers confronted by three potential penalty takers more often jumped into the correct goal corner. Whenever penalty takers did not try to deceive penalty takers, they could actually save more penalty kicks (compared to before their training, and even compared to other groups). Finding out which of the penalty takers actually will carry out the penalty kick turns attention to the parts of the penalty taker's movement execution that allow prediction of kick direction (without information overload). With time, goalkeepers gain a feel for how they can read certain information from the penalty taker's behavior without instructions.

Figure 20. An example of goalkeepers' gaze movement during a penalty shootout (taken from Dicks, Button, & Davids, 2010).

REFERENCES

Dicks, M., Button, C., & Davids, K. (2010). Examination of gaze behaviors under in situ and video simulation task constraints reveals differences in information pickup for perception and action. *Attention, Perception & Psychophysics, 72,* 706-720.

Dicks, M., Pocock, C., Thelwell, C. T., & van der Kamp, J. (2016). A novel on-field training intervention improves novice goalkeeper penalty kick performance. DOI: 10.1123/tsp.2015-0148.

21

Should the goalkeeper delay the penalty kick for as long as possible?

Many of us can still remember the 2015 DFB Cup semi-final, with FC Bayern Munich facing off against Borussia Dortmund. The winner had to be decided on penalty kicks, in this case a penalty shootout to remember. Dortmund won after Manuel Neuer, the fourth penalty taker for Bayern Munich, hit the goal post. Prior to Neuer's miss, Philip Lahm and Xabi Alonso slipped away during their attempts, and Mario Götze's penalty kick was saved by BVB goalkeeper Mitch Langerak. However, the most interesting moment was the penalty kick attempt of the former German National team's captain, Philip Lahm. Langerak was able to keep Lahm waiting for 40 seconds at the penalty spot by setting the water bottle aside and cleaning the shoes at the goal post. Does this long delay before the penalty kick make the penalty taker nervous?

Based on an analysis of penalty shootouts at FIFA World Championships, UEFA European Championships, and in the UEFA Champions League, the answer is yes. If a penalty taker had to wait longer for the referee's signal before starting his run toward the ball, the percentage of misses was higher than when the penalty takers had a shorter waiting time. There are no indications stating that it mattered who or what caused the delay. The general conclusion was that additional consideration time negatively affects the penalty taker, who normally is under extreme pressure and does not want to remain in this position for a long time.

However, the goalkeeper delaying the game does not affect all penalty takers in the same way and does not affect some players at all. Many well-known penalty takers want to quickly get it over with (sometimes with negative effects when they don't take their time for the penalty kick). These could become even more conscious of what is on the line if the goalkeeper delays the game. If a goalkeeper is additionally able to draw the penalty takers attention (more than necessary and useful), then this has a positive effect for the goalkeeper. Subsequent penalty kick attempts are often easier to save because they tend to end more in the direction of the goalkeeper. Goalkeepers seem to be aware of this, as in many cases they commit to a corner later during the run-up, which can be beneficial for shots that are not well placed. To conclude, goalkeepers should make use of such "mind games," even while aware that such effects may not be very big and that not every penalty taker can be influenced. Furthermore, there is a very thin line between influencing penalty takers and unfair behavior.

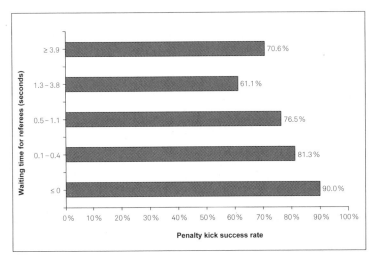

Figure 21. Relationship between the time which a penalty taker has to wait (here: the referee's ok) and his performance at the penalty kick (from Jordet et al., 2009).

REFERENCES

Furley, P., Dicks, M., Stendtke, F., & Memmert, D. (2012). "Get it out the way. The wait's killing me." Hastening and hiding during soccer penalty kicks. *Psychology of Sport and Exercise, 13*, 454-465.

Furley, P., Noël, B., & Memmert, D. (2016). Attention towards the goalkeeper and distraction during penalty shootouts in association football: a retrospective analysis of penalty shootouts from 1984 to 2012. *Journal of Sport Sciences.* DOI: 10.1080/02640414.2016.1195912

Jordet, G., Hartman, E., & Sigmunstad, E. (2009). Temporal links to performing under pressure in international soccer penalty shootouts. *Psychology of Sport and Exercise, 10*, 621-627.

22

Should the goalkeeper draw the penalty taker's attention to himself?

Goalkeepers sometimes come up with curious ways to attract the penalty taker's attention. Two examples: 1) During the penalty shootout of the 2015 DFB Cup semi-final between FC Bayern Munich and Borussia Dortmund, Mats Hummels headed to the penalty spot as the third penalty taker. Manuel Neuer tried to distract him by constantly jumping up and down and was then able to save Hummels's shot. 2) The first quarter-final match of the 2004 European Championship between Portugal and England went down in soccer history because of its drama. It was certainly not an evening for the faint-hearted. When the score was 2-2, after 120 minutes of play, it came down to the final penalty shootout, which was a miracle and no real surprise. England lost, allowing Portugal to reach the semi-final as it had four years prior.

There was pure excitement during both the regular and extra game time. Postiga leveled Owen's early leading goal shortly before the end of regular game time. In extra time, Rui Costa put the Portuguese ahead; then, Lampard's equalizer led England to the penalty shootout. However, they lost with a one-goal difference. With Hollywood-level drama, Beckham missed, his shot going embarrassingly high over the goal, and then there was 1-0 by Deco, a 1-1 by Owen with a bad flat shot to the center, 2-1 by Simao, and 2-2 by Lampard who also shot poorly to the center. Rui Costa then fired the ball with a speed of seemingly 200 kilometers per hour over the goal. 2-3 Terry, 3-3 C. Ronaldo, 3-4 Hargreaves, 4-4 Maniche, 4-5 Cole, 5-5 Helger Postiga. After that, the icing on the cake was Ricardo's performance. He returned to the goal without his gloves, hogged the limelight, and saved Vassell's shot, grabbing the ball and converting the following penalty kick by himself to reach 6-5. Does such behavior from the goalkeeper make the penalty takers nervous as their attention has been drawn from making the shot?

Scientific research considers what happens if penalty takers involuntarily give too much attention to the goalkeeper. How goalkeepers try to come by this is of secondary importance. It can even happen that coaches direct their players' attention unintentionally to the goalkeeper by instructing their players to ignore the goalkeeper. Basically, this can be imagined by somebody saying, "Don't think of the green elephant!" This automatically causes you to imagine a green elephant. However, based on various study results, it can be said that too much attention to the goalkeeper while carrying out a penalty kick is bad.

The fact is that goal-oriented actions, such as a penalty kick, always drift a little into the direction in which someone (here, the penalty taker) looks. If a penalty taker pays too much attention to a goalkeeper, then his kick often tends to be heading in the direction of the goalkeeper, at least more than intended. These kicks are then normally easier to save. But, of course, there are good reasons to pay more attention to a goalkeeper, such as when making use of a keeper dependent strategy to react to the goalkeeper's actions. However, you should be familiar with the risks beforehand.

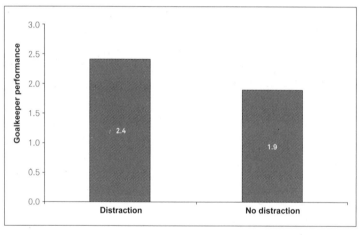

Figure 22. Goalkeeper performance when the goalkeeper tries to distract the penalty taker and when he does not. Values on the y-axis refer to the performance index according to Dicks et al., 2010 (maximal points when the goalkeeper saves the ball: 5; minimal points when the goalkeeper jumps into the wrong corner: 0).

REFERENCES

Bakker, F. C., Oudejans, R. D., Binsch, O., & van der Kamp, J. (2006). Penalty taking and gaze behavior: Unwanted effects of the wish not to miss. *International Journal of Sport Psychology*, 37, 265-280.

Binsch, O., Oudejans, R. D., Bakker, F.C., & Savelsbergh, G. J. P. (2010b). Ironic effects and final target fixation in a penalty shooting task. *Human Movement Science*, 29, 277-288.

Furley, P., Noël, B., & Memmert, D. (2016). Attention towards the goalkeeper and distraction during penalty shootouts in association football: a retrospective analysis of penalty shootouts from 1984 to 2012. *Journal of Sport Sciences*. DOI: 10.1080/02640414.2016.1195912

Wilson, M. R., Chattington, M., Marple-Horvat, D. E., & Smith, N. C. (2007) A comparison of self-focus versus attentional explanations of choking. *Journal of Sport & Exercise Psychology*, 29, 439-456.

23

Should the goalkeeper make use of deceptive movements?

The Women's World Cup between Japan and the US on July 17, 2011, was a historical event for Japanese women's soccer. Despite clear advantages of the Americans, a penalty shootout ultimately had to decide between victory and defeat. The Japanese goalkeeper, Ayumi Kaihori was able to save two penalty kicks, and US midfielder Carli Lloyd shot the ball over the goal. With the third converted penalty kick by defender Saki Kumagi, Japan's national women's soccer team won the World Champion title. Throughout the whole penalty shootout, Ayumi Kaihori did not try to deceive penalty takers and nevertheless succeeded. But there are other examples in which deceptions seem to work quite well.

In the 2005 Champions League final, Liverpool FC against AC Milan, the Liverpool goalkeeper, Jerzy Dudek, made small and quick movements from left to right, while also moving his arms jerkily during the second penalty kick for Milan. Andrea Pirlo was distracted by his behavior and completely missed the goal.

During the fourth penalty kick at the second leg of the 2012 Champions League semi-final, Real Madrid against FC Bayern Munich, Manuel Neuer repeatedly threw his arms in the air, as if someone had shouted, "hands up!" As a result, the Spanish player, Sergio Ramos, missed the goal, and after the next converted penalty kick by Schweinsteiger, the Bundesliga team won 4-3. The resulting question is, whether goalkeepers should make deceptive movements just before and during the penalty taker's run-up.

This question cannot be answered completely independently from the taker's penalty kick strategy. When penalty takers want to ignore the goalkeeper because they have already decided in which direction they want to shoot the ball, deceptive movements can still influence the player and keep him from carrying out his plan or make him nervous. However, a greater effect of deceptive movement is expected from a penalty taker who wants to observe a goalkeeper in order to subsequently kick to the side that the goalkeeper has not yet committed to. While running toward the ball, at some point these players have to decide in which direction they want to kick the ball. This usually occurs when they are sure that the goalkeeper will jump into one specific corner. Deceptive movements can make it extremely difficult for penalty takers to figure out what corner the goalkeeper plans to defend. Here, it is important that the penalty taker decides to go for one corner early, as they cannot interrupt their run-up completely and still need approximately 500 ms to shoot. In stressful situations such as an important penalty kick, it takes even longer. Thus, if a goalkeeper times his deceptive movements well (e.g., through feinting a specific direction in the right moment) and causes the penalty taker to react to the wrong movement, it can deliver a decisive advantage. However, one needs to be aware that only a minority of penalty takers try to react to the goalkeeper's movements and goalkeepers must still have enough time to carry out a final jump.

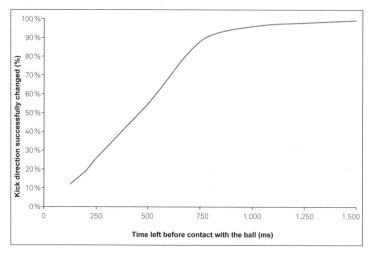

Figure 23. Percentage of penalty kicks during which the kick direction can still be changed successfully in relation to the time which is left before the penalty taker reaches the ball. If the goalkeeper deceives the penalty taker at the right moment, then he no longer has enough time to change the kicking direction successfully (taken from van der Kamp, 2006).

REFERENCES

Navarro, M., Miyamoto, N., van der Kamp, J., Morya, E., Ranvaud, R., & Savelsbergh, G. J. P. (2012). The effects of high pressure on the point of no return in simulated penalty kicks. *Journal of Sports & Exercise Psychology*, 34, 83-101.

Van der Kamp, J. (2006). A field simulation study of the effectiveness of penalty kick strategies in soccer: Late altercations of kick direction increase errors and reduce accuracy. *Journal of Sport Sciences*, 24, 467-477.

Bowtell, M., King, M. A., & Pain, M. T. G. (2009) Analysis of the keeper-dependent strategy in the soccer penalty kick. International Journal of Sport Sciences and Engineering, 3, 93-102.

Lees, A., & Nolan, L. (1998). The biomechanics of soccer: A review. *Journal of Sport Sciences*, 16, 211-234.

24

Should the goalkeeper position in the center of the goal?

Based on scientific evaluations of many penalty shootouts, there is a 93% chance that the goalkeeper does not stand right in the middle of the goal. This could perhaps be because it is not easy to find, or is just pure strategy. This was especially impressive during the penalty shootout between Switzerland and Ukraine at the FIFA World Cup 2006 in Germany. During the penalty shootout, the Ukrainian goalkeeper never stood directly in the middle of the goal. Facing Swiss penalty taker, Marco Streller, he was standing to the far left and was able to make a save. Can goalkeepers improve their chances by standing somewhat off-center? And if so, is there an influence on the penalty taker's goal-side selection?

Scientific studies confirm that goalkeepers can unconsciously influence the penalty taker by intentionally standing some centimeters to the left or right of the goal's center. In one study,

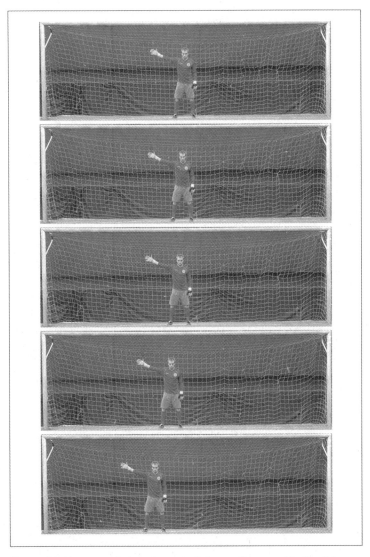

Figure 24. Five out of nine pictures of the goalkeeper with the right arm outstretched are presented. The goalkeeper was shown in a neutral goalkeeper posture, either in the middle of the goal, or in one of four off-center positions to the left (not shown here), or to the right.

the influence of the goalkeeper's gestures and position on the goal line on the penalty takers' goal side selection were tested. Soccer experts and novices had to carry out 54 penalty kicks and were confronted with goalkeepers in various positions and using different gestures.

The results are stunning. The already marginal displacement of the goalkeeper to the right or left (about 10 cm)—though penalty takers were not aware of it—makes penalty takers kick more often to the bigger side of the goal. That is, without being able to tell that there is a bigger goal side, penalty takers choose the bigger side in 60 to 75% of all cases!

This effect is more common in soccer experts, where the goalkeeper will additionally point to the bigger corner. Thus, every goalkeeper can theoretically influence a penalty taker by making use of the off-center effect to at least increase the probability of diving to the right goal side. A recommendation for the player in the goal is to stand less than 10 centimeters to one side of the goal's center to (unconsciously) offer the other side to the penalty taker. Jump into this corner right on time, and you will increase the chance of making a save, or at least of jumping into the correct corner.

REFERENCES

Masters, R. S. W., van der Kamp, J., & Jackson, R. C. (2007). Imperceptibly off-center goalkeepers influence penalty-kick direction in soccer. *Psychological Science, 18*, 222-223.

Noël, B., van der Kamp, J., & Memmert, D. (2015). Implicit goalkeeper influences on goal side selection in representative penalty kicking tasks. *PLoS ONE, 10*, e01354423.

Noël, B., van der Kamp, J., Weigelt, M., & Memmert, D. (2015). Asymmetries in spatial perception are more prevalent under explicit than implicit attention. *Consciousness and Cognition, 34*, 10-15.

Noël, B., van der Kamp, J., Masters, R., & Memmert, D. (2016). Scan direction influences explicit but not implicit perception of a goalkeeper's position. *Attention, Perception & Psychophysics.* DOI: 10.3758/s13414-016-1196-2

Weigelt, M., Memmert, D., & Schack, T. (2012). Kick it like Ballack: The effects of goalkeeping gestures on goal-side selection in experienced soccer players and soccer novices. *Journal of Cognitive Psychology, 24*, 942-956.

25

Should the goalkeeper try to anticipate the kick direction?

Although this sounds like a trivial question, goalkeepers who are able to do this especially well have a decisive advantage and can probably become the match-winner more often. Exactly this happened on March 20, 2010, when the players of Turbine Potsdam made history. With a 7-6 win in the penalty shootout against the French Champion Olympique Lyon, FFC Turbine secured the first UEFA Champions League title in women's soccer. When the match could not be decided in the regular playtime, a winner had to be determined from the penalty shot. After an outstanding performance by FFC goalkeeper, Anna Felicitas Sarholz, who saved two penalty kicks and converted one herself, the decision came with the 18th penalty kick which France's Elodie Thomis's kick hit the crossbar.

Theoretically, anticipating the shooting direction gives a decisive advantage to the goalkeeper. In actuality, he has far too little time (as a rule, less than half a second) to save a well-aimed shot if he just tries to react after the penalty taker touched the ball. This implies that a goalkeeper is often dependent on certain aspects, which provide him with information about the penalty taker's intentions (e.g., kick direction). These aspects can be visible very early in the penalty kick process like in the penalty taker's run-up angle or his gaze behavior prior to the run-up, or alternatively, shortly before the penalty taker touches the ball. The orientation of the non-kicking leg (pointing direction = kicking direction) and the angle of trunk and upper body can help to identify the penalty taker's intentions.

Early and late aspects of the penalty taker's behavior each have advantages and disadvantages. Early aspects allow the goalkeeper plenty of time to react to them, but they are relatively unreliable if penalty takers use deceptive movements. The late aspects are more reliable, but there is little time to react to them. On which aspects of penalty taker's behavior should a goalkeeper focus on to anticipate kick direction? It is not completely clear. The orientation of the penalty taker's non-kicking leg could be a good compromise of very early and very late stimuli for some goalkeepers. Compared to bad goalkeepers, good goalkeepers usually wait relatively long before reacting. They probably prefer to make use of late cues as well. However, being able to make use of these requires speed, elasticity, and agility.

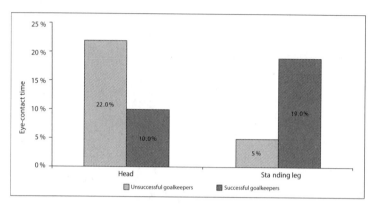

Figure 25. An overview of successful and unsuccessful goalkeepers (from Savelsbergh et al., 2005).

REFERENCES

Dicks, M., Button, C., & Davids, K. (2010). Availability of advance visual information constrains association goalkeeping performance during penalty kicks. *Perception*, 39, 1111-1124.

Savelsbergh, G. J. P., van der Kamp, J., Williams, A. M., & Ward, P. (2005). Anticipation and visual search behaviour in expert soccer goalkeepers. *Ergonomics*, 48, 1686-1697.

Loffing, F., Burmeister, T. & Hagemann, N. (2010). Zum Einfluss des Anlaufwinkels und des Schussfußes eines Schützen auf die Vorhersage der Ballflugrichtung beim Elfmeter. In G. Amesberger, T. Finkenzeller, & S. Würth (Eds.), Psychophysiologie im Sport – zwischen Experiment und Handlungsoptimierung (p. 132). Hamburg: Czwalina.

Should the goalkeeper commit to one side shortly before the penalty taker reaches the ball?

A huge effort was accomplished by the players of the US women's national team in the dramatic quarter-final match against Brazil on July 10, 2011. Brazil led 2-1 (and one of the US players was sent off) until US striker Abby Wambach equalized in the 122nd minute of play. The heroine of the penalty shootout, however, was goalkeeper Hope Solo who had good timing during the penalty kick attempt of Brazil's defender Daiane and was able to stop the ball. US defender, Ali Krieger then converted her penalty kick, as did her four teammates previously. Conspicuously, Brazilian goalkeeper, Andréia Suntaque, always clapped excessively before the opposing penalty taker's run-up.

If a reaction is performed shortly before the kicker makes contact with the ball, it is not easy because the goalkeeper's behavior or timing is, as already mentioned, determined essentially by his agility. More agile goalkeepers can take their time to initiate a movement. They can try to deceive the penalty taker quite late during his run-up and can gather more information about the penalty taker's intended actions (like the kick direction). Less agile goalkeepers have to take their physical preconditions into account and move to one corner earlier in order to ever have a chance to reach a more or less well-placed shot. It makes no difference with respect to time (only a matter of seconds), but there are certainly reasons for why successful goalkeepers commit to one side later than those with worse percentages. However, the goalkeeper's timing also needs to consider the penalty taker's strategic approach. If penalty takers try to react to the goalkeeper, it makes sense to wait a long time because a penalty taker must make his choice during his run-up to the ball. His time is running out, which can lead to imprecise penalty kicks.

However, if a penalty taker previously chose a corner, it can be advantageous to jump earlier. In this case, the penalty taker will not react to what the goalkeeper does, but instead has to change his strategy (which also implies certain risks during the run-up), giving the goalkeeper the opportunity to reach better-placed balls. However, the goalkeeper still has to perceive the direction in which the penalty taker is going to kick, based on scouting information or his own ability to anticipate kick direction correctly. Anticipation is more precise because the more information gathered, the longer the goalkeeper waits. The goalkeeper is stuck in a certain situation here. Due to his physical state and the penalty taker's behavior, he is forced to adapt his timing. That is not easy and is probably another reason why it is worth practicing saving penalty kicks. Perhaps this may as well be a reason for why some goalkeepers like Roman Weidenfeller seem to get better at saving penalty kicks steadily in the course of their career.

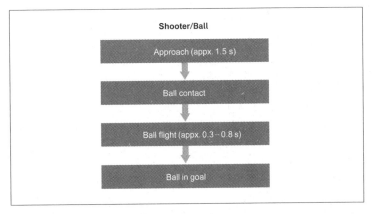

Figure 26. The temporal sequence of the penalty kick performance. From this, it can be recognized at which point in time the goalkeeper has, and how much time he has, to perform a defending movement (from Neumaier et al., 1987).

REFERENCES

Dicks, M., Davids, K., & Button, C. (2010). Individual differences in the visual control of intercepting a penalty kick is association football. *Human Movement Science*, 29, 401-411.

Neumaier, A. te Poel, H.-D. & Standtke, V. (1987). Zur Antizipation des Elfmeterschusses aus Sicht des Torhüters. *Leistungssport,* 17, 23-32.

Noël, B., & van der Kamp, J. (2006). Gaze behaviour during the soccer penalty kick: An investigation of the effects of strategy and anxiety. *International Journal of Sport Psychology,* 43, 326-345.

Savelsbergh, G. J. P., van der Kamp, J., Williams, A. M., & Ward, P. (2005). Anticipation and visual search behaviour in expert soccer goalkeepers. Ergonomics, 48, 1686-1697.

27

Should the goalkeeper avoid movements at the end of the penalty taker's run-up?

In contrast to the last chapter, it is also possible to ask if the goalkeeper should avoid making unnecessary movements and whether this can confuse the penalty taker. A good example for this is the behavior of Iker Casillas. During a penalty kick, he was known to stand on the goal line and barely move. Although he was a world-class goalkeeper, as long-term goalkeeper for Real Madrid and the Spanish national team, he has a poor record in penalty shootouts (9.09% saved penalty kicks). However, there were two German world-class goalkeepers that were just as well-known for standing relatively still in the center of the goal during penalty shootouts as they waited for the kick: Oliver Kahn and Jens Lehmann. Both goalkeepers, however, had a relatively good record of saved penalty kicks with 18.52% and 22.22%, respectively. In fact, the three saved penalty kicks by Oliver Kahn in the penalty shootout at the Champions League final in Milan in

2001 are still remembered today. Because of his heroics, Bayern Munich won versus FC Valencia in penalty kicks (5-4). However, what do we know about the advantages and disadvantages of this kind of goalkeeper behavior?

This question is not easy to answer and also depends on the penalty taker's behavior. If the penalty taker is to react to the goalkeeper's movement, it seems a good idea to reveal as little about one's own intentions as possible. However, even when not moving at all, the penalty taker is able to read into this. Most commonly, he would think that the goalkeeper will not be able to reach a well-placed ball, because of having to jump at an early point (this in turn is dependent on agility and other physical prerequisites). Thus, one should not linger motionless for too long. This means that even when successful goalkeepers start moving into one corner late, there is always a too-late point to begin moving. This is emphasized by the results of a penalty shootout analysis of the FIFA World Cups and UEFA European Championships from 1984-2012. According to this research, goalkeepers waited a long time before they began to move. Goalkeepers who waited too long, however, were less successful. In the case of saved penalty kicks, the goalkeepers jumped approximately 217 m before the penalty taker's foot–ball contact; in the case of converted penalty kicks approximately 172 m before foot–ball contact.

Furthermore, there is an experimental study which emphasizes that penalty takers moving back and forth draw more attention than static goalkeepers. Thus, it makes sense to move in the early phases of the run-up. Goalkeepers who consciously stand still have less influence on the penalty taker than those who move. They do without deceptions and distractions and thus put themselves in a more passive role than necessary.

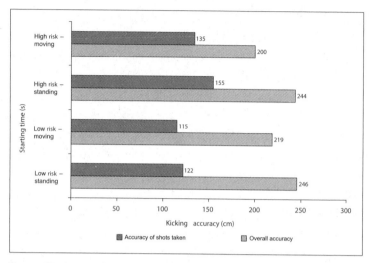

Figure 27: Moving benefits goalkeepers. This counts for pressure situations (high risk) as well as for experimental control situations (low risk).

REFERENCES

Dicks, M., Davids, K., & Button, C. (2010). Individual differences in the visual control of intercepting a penalty kick is association football. *Human Movement Science*, 29, 401-411.

Furley, P., Noël, B., & Memmert, D. (2016). Attention towards the goalkeeper and distraction during penalty shootouts in association football: a retrospective analysis of penalty shootouts from 1984 to 2012. *Journal of Sport Sciences*. DOI: 10.1080/02640414.2016.1195912

Savelsbergh, G. J. P., van der Kamp, J., Williams, A. M., & Ward, P. (2005). Anticipation and visual search behavior in expert soccer goalkeepers. *Ergonomics,* 48, 1686-1697.

Wood, G. & Wilson, M. R. (2010). A moving goalkeeper distracts penalty takers and impairs shooting accuracy. *Journal of Sport Sciences*, 28, 937-946.

28

Should the goalkeeper sometimes remain in the middle of the goal?

We all remember the fascinating FIFA World Cup final between Italy and France in 2006. After 120 minutes, the score was 1-1. After the penalty shootout, the Squadra Azzurra became World Champion, winning 5-3 when Trezeguet was the only player unable to convert his penalty kick. But what is it that sticks in your memory? Of course, there was the overtime during which not much momentous happened. But we did see Zidane, currently coach of Real Madrid, receive a red card after head-butting Materazzi. After seven minutes of regular game time, France's player Henry passed the ball to Malouda, who had entered the Italian penalty area and was slightly touched on the knee by Materazzi. Zidane converted the due penalty kick by kicking the ball into the middle of the goal with a cheeky lob shot, while Buffon jumped into the left corner. Just imagine if Buffon had stayed in the middle of the goal instead. He probably would have blocked the penalty kick, leaving Zidane standing there, looking pretty stupid. Just like Franck Ribery against Jens Lehmann (https://www.youtube.com/watch?v=UnMgfLwU0xU).

Based on analyses of 286 penalty shootouts in top national leagues and the UEFA Champions League, scientists concluded that a very effective strategy for goalkeepers would be to remain in the middle of the goal instead of going for one corner. In 29% of all penalty kicks, the penalty taker kicked the ball toward the middle of the goal. However, the goalkeepers, with few exceptions (6%), jumped either to the left or right corner, probably because of the misleading feeling that they had to do something to increase their chances. If goalkeepers remained in the middle, they would have a chance of holding high shots in the direction of the middle of the goal (at least if these shots were not kicked too hard). But they should indeed be able to stop a majority of shots that were kicked low or at middle height.

This strategy needs to be restricted because remaining in the middle is only a good idea for as long as the penalty taker does not expect this from the goalkeeper. If the player, however, does come to expect this, it provides the penalty taker with an advantage. The trick for the goalkeeper is to choose the optimal mix of different actions and be unpredictable. Remaining in the middle occasionally is part of the game, making it more difficult for the penalty taker to predict the intentions of the goalkeeper. He then has to expect not only two but three possible actions. This has less impact on penalty takers employing a keeper independent strategy, but it does makes it more difficult for penalty takers using a keeper dependent strategy.

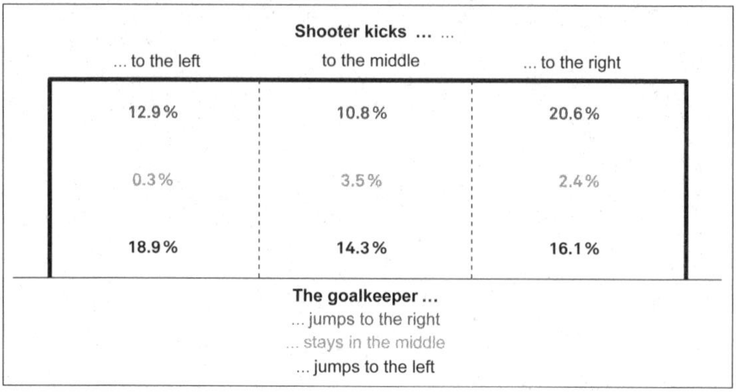

Shooter kicks		
... to the left	to the middle	... to the right
12.9%	10.8%	20.6%
0.3%	3.5%	2.4%
18.9%	14.3%	16.1%

The goalkeeper ...
... jumps to the right
... stays in the middle
... jumps to the left

Figure 28: Distribution of kick direction and direction of goalkeeper movement.

REFERENCES

Bar-Eli, A., Azar, O. H., Ritov, I., Keidar-Levin, Y., & Schein, G. (2007). Action bias among elite soccer goalkeepers: The case of penalty kicks. *Journal of Economic Psychology*, 28, 606-621.

Should the goalkeeper commit to the left side if the penalty taker is right-footed?

FC Bayern Munich won the 2015 German Cup quarter-final at Bayer Leverkusen with 5-3 in penalty kicks after Josip Drmic failed to score against Manuel Neuer. There were no goals during the 120 minutes. Bayern coach Pep Guardiola encouraged his team to perform as usual with high ball possession (73%); however, both teams were given several chances to score a goal. During extra time, Bayern should have been in a leading position, but Mario Götze missed the goal after Rafina passed him the ball. For this chapter, however, it is important that we look at the duel from the fifth penalty kick: Bernd Leno against Xabi Alonso. The right-footed Alonso chose the right goal corner; Leno jumped toward the right side of the goal but was not able to reach the ball in time.

The situation with Xabi Alonso is difficult to dissect because he is a player able to perform well with both his right and left feet. Having said that, he does generally take his penalty kicks with his right foot. In terms of the goalkeeper's performance, it's important to consider the kicking leg of the penalty taker. In different analyses, it was pointed out that penalty takers who kick with their right foot shoot more often toward the left than the right side (from the perspective of the penalty taker), and penalty takers who kick with their left foot shoot more often to the right than left side (also from the perspective of the penalty taker). Goalkeepers seem to be aware of this because they tend to jump toward the preferred corner of the goal for both left- and right-footed players.

However, penalty takers as well as goalkeepers have to be careful about becoming easily predictable, and therefore should try to change their behaviors and movements. Using game theory, a theory primarily used in economics, it can be described how frequently a penalty kicker should shoot to the left or the right side and how often a goalkeeper should jump to the left or the right (in relation to the kicking leg of the penalty taker). It is said that penalty takers kick toward their favorite corner (right-footed scorers toward the left side, and left-footed toward the right side) or that goalkeepers jump into the favorite corner of the penalty taker. However, this the player, be it the goalkeeper or the kicker, should only play this way as long as the opponent remains uncertain about his intentions. This means, penalty takers should aim for their preferred corner in 61% of all cases, and goalkeepers should jump toward this corner in 58% of the cases. Interestingly enough, this is almost exactly how goalkeepers and scorers play during competitions.

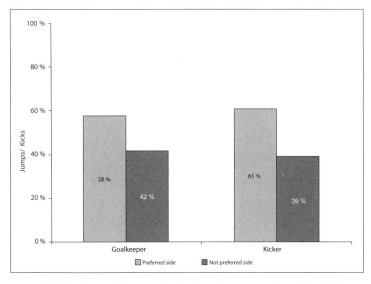

Figure 29. Perfect goalkeeper behavior based on game theory (see Palacios-Huerta, 2003).

REFERENCES

Chiappori, P.-A., Levitt, S., & Groseclose, T. (2002). Testing mixed-strategy equilibria when players are heterogeneous: The case of penalty kicks in soccer. *The American Economic Review*, 92, 1138-1151.

Palacios-Huerta, I. (2003). Professionals play mimimax. *Review of Economic Studies*, 70, 395-415.

Williams, A. M., & Burwitz, L. (1993). Advance cue utilization in soccer. In T. Reilly, J. Clarys & A. Stibbe (Eds.), Science and football II (pp. 239-243). London: E & FN Spon.

Should the goalkeeper focus on where the penalty taker hits the ball?

Marwin Hitz was responsible for causing a scandal during the game against FC Köln (the 15th match day, 2015/16), as he manipulated the field before Anthony Modeste carried out his penalty kick. While the Augsburg team ran toward referee Daniel Siebert to complain about his decision to award a penalty kick, the Augsburg goalkeeper went to the penalty spot. He dug the studs of his shoes into the ground and loosened it so that Anthony Modeste later slipped on the loose ground with his non-kicking leg, allowing Hitz to easily save the penalty. During the penalty kick attempt, Hitz seemed very determined and focused on the ball.

Focusing on where the penalty taker kicks the ball can help to predict the kick direction (at least theoretically) and save the penalty kick. The good thing about it is that the predictive value of this aspect of the kicking movement is relatively high. If a penalty taker is right-footed and hits the ball on the right side, the right corner of the goal from his view is unlikely.

However, it is questionable whether goalkeepers should try to predict the kick direction based on information regarding the foot-to-ball contact of the penalty taker. After foot-to-ball-contact, a ball needs less than 500 milliseconds until it crosses the goal line from 11 meters (with ball speeds of 80-100 km/h). Taking into consideration that a goalkeeper needs approximately the same amount of time to decide on one side and carry out his movement, it is evident that a goalkeeper will be too late unless the ball has been badly placed.

Based on the agility of the goalkeeper, which among others determines at which time the goalkeeper should ideally jump, this problem can become even greater. Larger and heavier or slower goalkeepers reduce the radius in which they could reach the ball even more than agile goalkeepers when they wait that long to initiate their movement. This example points out that not all scientific results are directly transferable to the sport environment because this environment quite often differs from the environment in lab-based studies. Thus, in this case, studies only show the theoretical possibilities but not what should be done by goalkeepers in order to improve their chances.

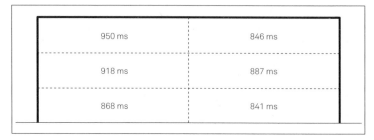

Figure 30. Movement time (in milliseconds) for each goalkeeper. Destination: participant/player (from Dicks et al. 2010).

REFERENCES

Dicks, M., Davids, K., & Button, C. (2010). Individual differences in the visual control of intercepting a penalty kick in association football. Human Movement Science, 29, 401-411.

Lees, A. & Owens, L. (2011). Early visual cues associated with a directional place kick in soccer. *Sports Biomechanics*, 10, 125-134.

Memmert, D., Hüttermann, S., Hagemann, N., Loffing, F., & Strauss, B. (2013). Dueling in the penalty box: evidence-based recommendations on how penalty takers and goalkeepers can win penalty shootouts in soccer. *International Review of Sport and Exercise Psychology*, 6, 209-229.

Neumaier, A., te Poel, H.-D., & Standtke, V. (1987). Zur Antizipation des Elfmeterschusses aus der Sicht des Torhüters. *Leistungssport,* 17, 23-32.

31

Should the goalkeeper try to "look tall?"

Manuel Neuer is a very athletic and tall person. He is 1.93 meters (6 ft., 4 in.) tall and defends 77.78% of shots on the goal—a top result in the Bundesliga ranking 2015/16. There were only two people documented to be even better: Timo Horn (78.35%) and Koen Casteels (84.62%). However, and you should pay attention to this, Manuel Neuer makes himself appear even taller by jumping to touch the crossbar. Does this influence the kicker?

Researches from VU Amsterdam were able to show that the perceived height of a goalkeeper has the potential to influence the penalty taker. They analyzed different postures that a goalkeeper can assume, allowing him to appear taller or smaller. Without being able to name it, many people still know the Müller-Lyer illusion (after its founder, Franz Müller-Lyer). This is a geometrical, optical illusion consisting of a straight line, with an arrow being attached at both ends. The arrows on both ends of the straight lines either face toward the center of the straight line, or away from it. If the arrows on both sides point to the center, the straight line usually appears shorter to the viewer than it does when the arrows point to the outside, even though both lines have the same length.

Importantly, goalkeepers can make use of these illusions as well by spreading their arms over their head or downwards away from their body. The experiment of the scientific group in Amsterdam demonstrated that goalkeepers can make themselves appear 3-5% (ca. 5-10 cm) taller by spreading their arms up. Does this also have an effect on the behavior of the penalty taker? Here, the answer seems to be yes. In another experiment, it was shown that if the goalkeeper appears to be taller because of his body posture, the penalty taker aims for a target area farther away from the goalkeeper. The number of kicks missing the goal to the left or right side is also higher, but not significantly enough to note. For goalkeepers, it seems to make sense to appear taller or sometimes smaller in order to influence the scorer, and make penalty takers' behavior more predictable.

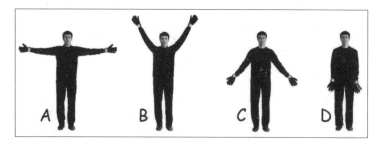

Figure 31. An overview of postures that allow goalkeepers to appear neutral (A), tall (B), or small (C).

REFERENCES

Van der Kamp, J., & Masters, R. S. W. (2007). The human Müller-Lyer illusion in goalkeeping. *Perception*, 37, 951-954.

32

Should the goalkeeper demonstrate happiness and pride after a successful save?

Can you still remember the legendary penalty shootout at the FIFA World Cup 2006? Of course, we are talking about the quarter-final of the German team against Argentina which took place in Berlin. In a highly competitive match with two headed goals by Roberto Ayala and Miroslav Klose, the game was still tied after 120 minutes. Shortly after the break, Argentina's defender Ayala gave his team the lead. However, right before the end of the game, Klose scored the equalizer with his fifth tournament goal. But after saving the penalty kicks of Esteban Cambiasso and Roberto Ayala, it was Jens Lehmann who became the hero. For the German team, Oliver Neuville, Michael Ballack, Tim Borowski, and Lukas Podolski scored. This is all known information, but there is a small detail missing. After Lehmann saved his second penalty kick, he did not jump joyfully around, but rather remained calm. This was untypical for such an important match and in general when one saves a second penalty kick. Do emotional breakouts of goalkeepers after saved penalty kicks matter, and if so, how do they matter? Can it even be an advantage to stay calm and not act euphorically?

From a scientific perspective, there are not enough resources available to answer this question. The only study on this topic analyzes all penalty shootouts in UEFA European Championships and FIFA World Cups between 1972 and 2008, mainly dealing with the joyful behavior of the penalty taker. As described, an effect of excessive joyful celebration can be demonstrated, but whether or not this can be transferred to the goalkeeper's behavior is unclear. Though it seems possible, there is currently no scientific evidence to support this claim. Furthermore, Lehmann behaved strikingly different from what penalty takers might have expected. This can divert the attention of the following penalty taker to the goalkeeper, which might benefit the goalkeeper. If one gets "into the head of the opposite player" by cheering, it makes no difference. The actual idea behind the influence of displaying emotions on the fellow and opposite player is known as emotional contagion. This is something that will certainly be the topic of future studies, hopefully also going on to involve the behavior and influence of goalkeepers on penalty takers.

REFERENCES

Moll, T., Jordet, G., & Pepping, G. (2010). Emotional contagion in soccer penalty shootouts: Celebration of individual success is associated with ultimate team success. *Journal of Sport Sciences*, 28, 983-992.

CREDITS

Cover design: Andreas Reuel
Interior design: Annika Naas
Layout: Zerosoft
Cover photo: © dpa

Managing editor: Elizabeth Evans
Copyeditor: Qurratulain Zaheer